Sam Siggs

Love Bites

Salamander Street

PLAYS

First published in 2021 by Salamander Street Ltd.
(info@salamanderstreet.com)

Love Bites © Sam Siggs, 2021

All rights reserved.

Application for professional and amateur performance rights should be directed to the author c/o Salamander Street. No performance may be given unless a licence has been obtained, and no alterations may be made in the title or the text of the adaptation without the author's prior written consent.

You may not copy, store, distribute, transmit, reproduce or otherwise make available this publication (or any part of it) in any form, or binding or by any means (print, electronic, digital, optical, mechanical, photocopying, recording or otherwise), without the prior written permission of the publisher. Any person who does any unauthorized act in relation to this publication may be liable to criminal prosecution and civil claims for damages.

ISBN: 9781914228391

10 9 8 7 6 5 4 3 2 1

Cast List

MALCOLM
GIRL (CUPID)
LEO
REMY
ELLIE
GRACE
DWAYNE
BRYONY
SCOTT
ANTHEA
DARYL
AMY
SHY BOY
PHONE GIRL
SIGN PERSON
HAPPY PERSON
MATT
WILL
OLIVER
SHELLEY
SADIE
COLETTE
JOE
MARK
QUENTIN
ASHLEY
ERICA
GEORGE
CHLOE

Love Bites was first performed on 17 June 2012 at the Scottish Storytelling Centre, Edinburgh.

The cast was David Avern, Daniel Crawford, Megan Donnachie, Archie Fisher, Reuben Gourlay, Tallulah Greive, Molly Harkins, Charlie Johnston, Mary Kemp Bruce, Danny Lamb, Emily Magee, Baillie McLean, Helena Moore, Rannoch Moore, Callum Neilson, Ellie Small, Alistair Stiven, Caeleb Wall

Director: Ruth Hollyman

Assistant Director: Lucy McGlennon

Written by Sam Siggs and commissioned and produced by Strange Town

Launched in 2008 Strange Town is a theatre company for young people. In that time Strange Town has commissioned and produced over 100 new plays by young emerging writers. These plays have been performed in venues throughout Edinburgh including; The Traverse Theatre, Lyceum Theatre, Scottish Storytelling Centre, Roxy Art House, Hill Street Theatre as well as underneath the East stand at Easter Road the home of Hibernian Football Club. Strange Town plays have also been performed in Scottish prisons, conferences and in secondary schools across Scotland.

For further information on Strange Town scripts email info@strangetown.org.uk or visit www.strangetown.org.uk

AUTHOR'S NOTE ON THE PLAYTEXT: The sex/gender of the characters in this version of the text were chosen to reflect that of the cast in the play's most recent production. Beyond that, the sex/gender of the characters is not fixed and I encourage directors to change/adapt this element of the text at their discretion. Character names are arbitrary and can be changed as the director and cast see fit.

The setting of the play is Edinburgh and, as such, the play references very specific Edinburgh locations. Please feel free to adapt these settings to reflect a production's performance location.

Midsummer's Night. Edinburgh. A **GIRL** *with plastic angel wings, a plastic bow and arrow and a sash with a big red 'L' for learner sign sits crying on a park bench.*

MALCOLM *enters with a bag of chips. He stops and eyes the distraught* **GIRL** *warily. Looks around to ascertain whether she's alone. She is. He approaches cautiously. A particularly loud sob makes him jump. He takes a step back.*

MALCOLM: Are you alright?

The **GIRL**, *suddenly aware of* **MALCOLM**, *grabs her bow and arrow and aims it at him.*

MALCOLM: Easy. No need for violence.

She shoots and misses.

GIRL: SHIT! Why do I always miss?!

MALCOLM: Would you like a chip?

GIRL: No, I would not like a chip. Unless it's a magical chip that can take away all the pain and suffering in the world.

MALCOLM: Just normal chips.

GIRL: In that case, piss off.

MALCOLM: But they do have cheese on them.

GIRL: Now yer talkin! Frickin GIES!!

Puts chip in her mouth and then spits it out in disgust.

GIRL: Mayonnaise!? Why would you do that? Could things actually get any worse?

MALCOLM: Bad night?

GIRL: Buddy you have no idea

MALCOLM: Come on. Things can't be that bad. Probably just a wee bit too much to drink, yes?

GIRL: I've had nowhere near enough to drink. I'm gonna keep on drinking until I forget how much of an epic failure I am. In fact, I'm gonna drink to the point where the words 'epic failure' have no meaning anymore on account of my brain having gone all mushy.

MALCOLM: Well I don't think that's a good idea.

GIRL: It's a terrible idea. But I'm doing it regardless.

MALCOLM: Y'know, these Hen Night things usually end up being quite emotional. Maybe you should just…

GIRL: I'm not on a hen night.

MALCOLM:. Then why are you dressed like Cupid?

GIRL: Uh… Because I am Cupid. Why else would I be dressed as Cupid? God.

MALCOLM: But isn't Cupid a little naked baby dude?

GIRL: No. No Cupid is not. Everyone always says that. No. I'm Cupid.

MALCOLM: Yeeeeeah no I'm pretty sure Cupid's a little naked baby dude.

GIRL: Look pally-wally, we're talking the God of Desire, here. Of Lust. Affection. Overpowering romantic erotic and all-the-shit-inbetween Love, mate. If I was a little naked baby dude it would be highly inappropriate.

MALCOLM: Spose it would be a bit dodge.

Pause.

MALCOLM: You don't look much like a God.

GIRL: Oh really now? And how many Gods have you met?

MALCOLM: Well…none.

GIRL: Exactly.

MALCOLM: If you're a God then why are you drunk…and crying…on a bench…?

GIRL: Being the God of Love is precisely the reason why I'm drunk and crying on a bench! It's a shit show! I mean, look, here we are. Midsummer's night. The balmy evening air should be filled with the blissful sighs of a million happy lovers. Like, the whole universe should be vibrating with the joyous ebb and flow of *(Weird jazz hands.)* LUUUURVE…

MALCOLM: That would be nice.

GIRL: Yeah it would be, wouldn't it? 'Cept all youse fannies have to keep making it so frickin complex.

MALCOLM: 'Youse fannies?' What?

GIRL: Humans.

Beat.

Like, I've been swooping about the place all day. Dishing out the love. But y'all can't seem to even handle that shit and quite frankly it's doing mah nut, right?

MALCOLM: Not following you, pal.

GIRL: Oh you will. Take a seat.

Pause.

Don't be shy, chip-boy.

MALCOLM *warily sits on the bench.*

GIRL: Close your eyes. Now. Let me show you just a couple of things I've had to deal with today.

MALCOLM *closes his eyes.* **CUPID** *kisses him on the forehead. Blackout.*

LOVE BITE #1

Bruntsfield Primary School. The playground. 10:32 am

LEO *and* **REMY** *are playing catch with a big red bouncy ball.* **REMY** *doesn't seem to be paying much attention to the game and keeps looking listlessly over his shoulder.*

LEO: Not allowed NERF guns in the playground anymore.

REMY: Whassat?

LEO: NERF guns. Y'know like 'pfoo!pfoo!pfoo!' *(Mimes.)* NERF guns.

REMY: Ooh! NERF guns!

LEO: NERF guns. Yeah. Not allowed them in the playground anymore.

REMY: Oh no.

LEO: Want to know why not?

REMY: Hm?

LEO: Want to know why not?

REMY: Think I maybe know 'why not'.

> **ELLIE** *enters, walking past briskly. She pauses. They abruptly stop playing bouncy ball. Look at the sky/at their feet.* **ELLIE** *exits.*

LEO: Yeahno. But if Michael Willoughby hadn't cried in the first place…

REMY: He's just a big cry baby is what he is.

LEO: Yes, he is one. He said Danny Murray shot him in the willy and that it hurt. But he's a big liar because I've been shot in the willy loads of times and it doesn't hurt at all.

REMY: Why have you been shot in the willy loads of times?

LEO: Duh! Because it's only, like, the whole point of the game!

REMY: Is it?

LEO: Course it is. But enough about Michael Willoughby's poopy ol willy. Michael Willoughby isn't the real problem, is he?

ELLIE *walks past again. They both freeze. She exits.*

REMY: Well there're lots of other games and things.

LEO: No. No there's not. We're not allowed to play paper airplanes anymore cos Emma Dickson got a paper cut on her eye. We're not allowed to play toilet tig anymore cos Miles Dempsey wet himself. We're not allowed to play hide and seek anymore cos no one could find 3P6. We're not allowed to play chess anymore because Jeremy Watson kept getting over excited and pulling his trousers down. We're not even allowed to play 'Trans-Siberian Death March' anymore.

REMY: *(Paying attention for the first time.)* WHAT?! No waaay-ah! Why not?

LEO: *(Scandalized.)* Mrs. Phillips. Wouldn't. Even. Say!

REMY: Well that's just rubbish.

LEO: Yeah. But, like, it wouldn't even…even be a thing…if someone wasn't such a big…

ELLIE *enters again.*

ELLIE: Hello Remy. Leo.

LEO/REMY: Ellie.

ELLIE: Whatcha doing?

LEO/REMY: Nothin'

ELLIE: That a bouncy ball?

LEO/REMY: No.

Pause.

ELLIE: Okay.

I'm going to go stand next to Mrs Phillips now.

ELLIE *exits.* **LEO** *begins to follow her.*

REMY: Leo. What you doing?

LEO: Gonna go push Ellie over. In the playground.

REMY: No don't! That's…naughty!

LEO: Yeah well, Snitches get stitches.

REMY: What's that mean?

LEO: Dunno. But it's troo.

REMY: Leo don't…we'll both get in trouble. And it'll just make things… badder.

LEO: OkayFine.
(Beat.)
Least we can still play bouncy ball.

REMY: Mm-hm.

LEO: I love bouncy ball. Don't you?

REMY: Uh-huh.

LEO: Ellie'll never get bouncy ball banned.

REMY: Oh yeah. No. Yeah. Mm-hm.

LEO: What you keep lookin at, Remy?

REMY: What? Nothin. No one. Shut up.

LEO: You definitely keep looking at something.

REMY: I don't. I'm not. And even if I did…or am…or was looking at something…well what's it to you, eh?

LEO: Do you want some of Grace Walker's Monster Munch? Is that why you keep looking at her like that?

REMY: Yeah, hmmph, well, aren't you going to look silly, because actually…actually…

LEO: GRACE! GRACE COME OVER HERE!

> **GRACE** *enters.* **REMY** *stares at the ground.*

GRACE: Hello Leo. Hello Remy.

LEO: Hi Grace. Can Remy have one of your Monster Munches please?

GRACE: Oh. I finished them all. Sorry.

LEO: Never mind then. Bye Grace.

GRACE: Bye Leo. Bye Remy.

She goes to leave.

REMY: *(Gabbling.)* NERF guns aren't allowed in the playground anymore because Dan Murray shot Michael Willoughby in the willy and Michael cried to Mrs Phillips about his willy and now NERF guns aren't allowed in the playground anymore.

GRACE: Pardon?

REMY: *(Gabbling.)* Nobody's allowed to shoot anyone in the willy with a NERF gun ever again even though that's the whole point of the game and even though it doesn't hurt anyway because Michael's just a big cry baby. Just… so's you know.

GRACE: Oh. *(Pause.)* Thanks Remy.

REMY: Um…Grace?

GRACE: Yes?

REMY: Would you…would you like to play bouncy ball with me and Leo?

GRACE: Oh yes please. I love bouncy ball.

LEO: Everyone loves bouncy ball!

REMY: Okay then! Catch!

__REMY__ throws the bouncy ball full force in __GRACE__'s face. Everyone is stunned. The shock wears off and __GRACE__ starts to cry. __ELLIE__ appears, as if from nowhere.

ELLIE: Saw that.

LEO: And now you're…

ELLIE: Telling. Yep. Mrs Phillips! Mrs Phillips!

LEO: No Ellie! Not bouncy ball! Please!

ELLIE *runs off.*

LEO: Why, Remy?!!

REMY: I'm sorry!!

LEO: You've ruined bouncy ball! Mrs Phillips is going to come running over with her clipboard and her shouting and her big nasty face and that will be the end of bouncy ball forever! Why Remy!? Why did you do it?

REMY: I don't know! I…I really don't know.

Blackout.

Midsummer's Night. The bench.

MALCOLM: Whoa!

CUPID: See that? First one of the day.

MALCOLM: You… really are a God

CUPID: Aye. All be it a crap one. You see how that went? Balls to the face before lunchtime. Start as you mean to go on, eh?

MALCOLM: Yeah but they were only wee. Give them a break.

CUPID: Spose. But believe me, youse fannies don't get any better at it with age. Keep watching.

LOVE BITE #2

ASKING PEOPLE OUT: A MONTAGE OF INEPTITUDE

BITE #2A

In an exam. 10.45am. **DWAYNE** *sits directly behind* **BRYONY**.

DWAYNE: Psst!

No reaction.

DWAYNE: Psst!

No reaction.

DWAYNE *throws a rubber at the back of her head.*

DWAYNE: Have you finished yet?

BRYONY: No you can't borrow my protractor. You should have brought your own.

DWAYNE: No…I'm saying have you finished?

BRYONY: Yes.

DWAYNE: What did you get for question three?

BRYONY: Not telling.

DWAYNE: Nah nah I've already done it like….just…y'know…shooting the shit.

BRYONY: Shoot someone else's shit. We're not supposed to be talking.

DWAYNE: Isn't it good that we don't have exams on a Saturday?

Silence.

DWAYNE: I like to keep my Saturdays free of exams.

Silence.

DWAYNE: My Saturday is free.

Silence.

DWAYNE: What's your Saturday looking like?

BRYONY: I am going to the cinema with my boyfriend.

Silence.

DWAYNE: I go to Greggs for lunch.

Pause.

DWAYNE: Gonna go again today.

Pause.

DWAYNE: Gonna get a steak bake.

Pause.

DWAYNE: And some Irn-Bru.

BRYONY: Please stop talking.

Pause.

DWAYNE: And a yum-yum.

BRYONY *sticks her hand in the air.*

DWAYNE: What you putting your hand up for?

Pause.

DWAYNE: Actually… can I borrow your protractor?

BRYONY: I do Judo you know.

BITE #2B

ANTHEA *is sitting reading the Metro newspaper in Snax cafe. 11.45am.* **SCOTT** *enters behind her. He checks his breath. It obviously stinks. He takes a packet of Trebor extra strong mints from his pocket. He takes one. Then another. Then another. Then another. Soon his mouth is full of mints. He crunches them noisily. He has underestimated how strong they are and splutters them all out all over the place.*

He practises how he's going to say 'Hi' silently behind her for a bit. He strolls up.

SCOTT: *(Squeaks.)* Hi! *(Affecting a manly deep voice.)* I mean Hi. Hi….Hi.

ANTHEA: Uh…Hi.

SCOTT: Is there anyone sitting here? Yes. Yes there is. I'm sitting here. This is me sitting here now. Beside you. Yes.

ANTHEA: Sit away.

SCOTT: You reading the paper yeah?

ANTHEA: No.

SCOTT: Ha! You're funny. What star sign are you?

ANTHEA: Why?

SCOTT: You'll be a Libra then. Inquisitive Libra. Always asking questions. Always asking 'why?' Seeking out the truth. 'Why?' 'Whyyyyyyy?'

ANTHEA: If you must know I'm a Scorpio.

SCOTT: Ah Scorpio! Of course! Fiery Scorpio! Beguiling Scorpio! Dirty, kinky, scandalous Scorpio!

ANTHEA: Are you going anywhere with this?

SCOTT: Yes. Let me read you your horoscope.

ANTHEA: I'd rather you didn't

Grabs the paper.

SCOTT: Says here you're going to meet a tall handsome stranger. Well… not that tall really…and not really a stranger either…Maybe someone who's in your Home Ec class.

ANTHEA: Let me see that.

SCOTT: It's unlucky to read your own horoscopes.

They wrestle over the paper. **SCOTT** *manages to chuck it into the audience.*

SCOTT: Oops.

They sit in silence.

SCOTT: Soooo. Do you like to do…stuff?

ANTHEA: No

SCOTT: I like to do stuff.

Pause.

How bout you and me. In the same place. Friday. Doin stuff. Whaddaya say?

ANTHEA: Okay. I'm geting the feeling that you like me.

SCOTT: Yeah! Yeah I do actually.

ANTHEA: Why?

SCOTT: You just seem like…a really cool person.

ANTHEA: What are you basing this on exactly?

SCOTT: I dunno. Just…yer eyes.

ANTHEA: My eyes.

*****SCOTT** nods.*

ANTHEA: Seriously?

He nods.

Oh you poor sweet thing. Okay.

She writes a number on a piece of paper and gives it to **SCOTT**.

SCOTT: Whoa, seriously?

ANTHEA: Laters.

She exits.

SCOTT: Wow. Lots of numbers in your number.

He waits for a second then whips out his phone and calls the number. It doesn't go through.

SCOTT: Must have her phone off.

BITE #2C

The commonwealth pool. A flume. 11.50am. **DARYL** *comes sliding down.*

DARYL: WHEEEEE!!

He grinds to a halt.

DARYL: Oh. Um. Wheeee.

Tries to wiggle himself unstuck again to no avail.

DARYL: Okay, think I might be..um..Wheee? Whee.

AMY *comes sliding down the flume and gets stuck directly behind* **DARYL**.

Silence.

DARYL: Hi.

AMY: Um…Hi.

DARYL: I'm stuck by the way.

AMY: Oh.

DARYL: You stuck?

AMY: Well yes.

DARYL: So we're both stuck. Both good 'n stuck.

AMY: It would appear so.

DARYL: Could be worse. My cousin Jamie said someone put razor blades in a flume in Fife once and some lady lost a whole bum cheek. Imagine that? Like, losing a bum cheek! I mean, what would you even sit on?

AMY: Well thankfully both my bum cheeks are fine.

DARYL: Yeah they are.

AMY: Pardon?

DARYL: Nothing!

AMY: Look. Can you not try and wiggle yourself free? I don't really want to spend the rest of the afternoon stuck in a water-filled tube.

DARYL: Again. Could be worse.

AMY: How?

DARYL: Could be stuck in some railings, or a lift that someone's peed in…or a haunted well.

AMY: Haunted well? What are you talking about?

DARYL: Haunted well! Like in that film 'The Ring'. The lassie with the hair and the googly eye gets all trapped in a haunted well and she's all like 'Naw!' and it looks well shan in the haunted well. Much better in here than in the haunted well.

AMY: Thanks for that. I shall steer clear of all haunted wells in the future.

DARYL: Solid plan.

Pause.

DARYL: So how's your swimming been so far, Amy?

AMY: Sorry. Do I know you?

DARYL: Convalescent bonds, Amy, Convalescent bonds.

AMY: What?

DARYL: It's me, Daryl, Amy. I sit behind you in chemistry.

AMY: Do you?

DARYL: *(Slightly hurt.)* 'Do you?' she says. Yes Amy I do. Do you not remember when I asked you what your favourite element was and you said 'zinc' and I said that 'potassium' is far superior to zinc because when you stick it in a Bunsen burner it goes all purple. Do you remember that little exchange?

AMY: Yeah. Now you mention it.

DARYL: Good time. Good times.

AMY: So, Daryl. Do you think we'll be stuck in here long?

DARYL: Naaaah. Once the lifeguards notice we haven't come out the other end they'll send a chubby kid down at breakneck speed to sort of flush us out. Don't you worry. We'll be out of here in no time.

Sometime later. (12.00pm.)

DARYL: I spy with my little eye something beginning with… 'F'.

AMY: Flume.

DARYL: Correct. Your go.

AMY: I spy with my little eye something beginning with… 'F'.

DARYL: Flume.

AMY: Yep.

DARYL: My go. I spy with my little eye something beginning with… 'F'.

AMY: Can we play something else now?

DARYL: How about imaginary I-spy? I imagine I've seen something and then you have to guess what it is.

AMY: Um…

Later still… (12.20pm)

DARYL: Y'know. If we weren't both wearing swimming costumes…we'd be naked.

AMY: Yes. Yes we would.

DARYL: Just something to think about.

Even later still. (12.50pm.)

   DARYL and **AMY** *sing 'Total Eclipse of the Heart' at the top of their lungs.*

AMY: God I love Bonnie Tyler.

DARYL: Another thing we've got in common.

Later…

DARYL: Actually quite cold now.

AMY: I've gone all wrinkly.

Pause.

AMY: Daryl…Do you think we're going to die here?

DARYL: More than likely.

AMY: Daryl….if we don't die…if by some miracle we make it out of here alive…would you like to do something after school one day?

DARYL: YES PLEASE! I mean…yeah, cool.

Silence.

DARYL *seems uncomfortable.*

AMY: Daryl? You okay?

DARYL: …

AMY: You've gone all quiet.

DARYL: Sorry. Just…wasn't expecting you to…y'know…

AMY: Oh.
Look, we don't have to hang out if you don't want to…

DARYL: It's not that. I do want to. Like, a lot…

AMY: What's wrong then?

DARYL: It's just…aaaaw man…

AMY: What?

DARYL: I don't know how to say this, Amy…

AMY: Say what, Daryl?

DARYL: It's just…I'm no actually stuck.

*Back on the bench with **MALCOLM** and **CUPID**.*

CUPID: Wasn't that just the cringeyiest display ever?

MALCOLM: I don't know. That last guy was quite the playa!

CUPID: That's playa behavior, is it? Pretending to be stuck in a flume?

MALCOLM: Points for creativity at least. Come on. Show me some more. I'm getting into this now.

LOVE BITE #3

Princes Street Gardens. A bench. 12:51 pm.

SHY BOY *and* **PHONE GIRL** *sit next to each other on the bench.*

PHONE GIRL *is deeply engrossed in the text message she is writing.*

SHY BOY *sits silently and nervously beside her.*

SHY BOY *takes a long and loving look at* **PHONE GIRL**.

PHONE GIRL *ignores him.*

SHY BOY *takes another look of longing and this time of pain.*

PHONE GIRL *ignores him.*

SHY BOY *takes one last look of longing and pain and opens his mouth to speak.*

PHONE GIRL *suddenly fixes him with a stony glare.*

SHY BOY *clams up and looks away.*

PHONE GIRL *goes back to her texting.*

LOVE BITE #4

North Bridge. 12:52 pm

SIGN PERSON *stands holding a sign which reads 'Jesus is Love, God hates Fags'.*

HAPPY PERSON *enters.*

HAPPY PERSON *stands next to* **SIGN PERSON**.

HAPPY PERSON *smiles at* **SIGN PERSON**.

HAPPY MAN *produces their own sign which reads:*

'I Love Jesus'.

SIGN PERSON *sees this and nods in approval.*

Pause.

HAPPY PERSON *drops sign to reveal another sign underneath which reads:*

'But nowhere near as much…'.

Pause.

HAPPY PERSON *drops sign to reveal a third sign which reads:*

'…as I love this guy'.

There is an arrow on the sign pointing to **SIGN PERSON**.

SIGN PERSON *looks very uncomfortable.*

Pause.

HAPPY PERSON *drops sign to reveal a fourth sign which reads:*

'Seriously…'

HAPPY PERSON *drops sign to reveal a final sign which reads:*

'PHWOAR!'.

SIGN PERSON *sees this and edges off stage.*

HAPPY PERSON *follows them.*

LOVE BITE #5

Matt's bedroom.

A knocking on the bedroom door.

MATT: Who is it?

WILL: Me.

MATT: Oh. Okay. Just a second…

    Beat.

WILL: Can I come in?

MATT: Just a second I said!

    MATT *jumps up off his bed and scans the room for anything incriminating.*

MATT: Okay you can come in now.

    MATT*'s older brother* **WILL** *enters.*

MATT: I was just…

WILL: Coolwhateverman. *(Beat.)* Matt?

MATT: Yeah?

WILL: Can we…talk?

MATT: What about?

    WILL *walks over to the bed, sits down.*

WILL: Take a seat.

MATT: What about, Will?

WILL: Just…take a seat, yeah?

    MATT *sits.*

WILL: It's about Jane.

MATT: Uh…Jane?

WILL: Come on, man. I know you know about Jane. Y'know, ever since you walked in on us…

MATT: Okaaaaydon'tneedtotalkaboutthatthankyooooo!

WILL: Alright! Alright. Just…Matt…You haven't, like, seen her about lately, have you?

MATT: No. Why d'you ask?

WILL: Well. It's just…she's sort of gone AWOL, pal. So…

MATT: So? So what?

WILL: So, I just thought…

MATT: Look Will. I am positive I've had zero contact with Jane… She's your girlfriend so…

WILL: Girlfriend? Come on. She was never my…I wouldn't say girlfriend, exactly.

MATT: Property then.

WILL: That is a horrible way to put it. Jane is nobody's property. She is –

MATT: 'A beautiful gift to the world.'

WILL: Exactly.

Just know right, if you had maybe….seen her. I wouldn't be angry or anything.

MATT: Okay?

WILL: Yeah, I wouldn't be angry. I'd understand.

MATT. Uh…understand what exactly?

WILL: *(Raises his eyebrows.)* Come on man, I've seen the way you look at her. And I'm just saying, that's fine. You're my brother. So no matter what…you'll always come first so…

MATT: *(Cooly.)* Okay, I think this conversation is over now.

WILL: Okay.

Okay that's…fine. Sorry to have disturbed you.

WILL *gets up to leave.*

Look I just want to know that she's okay, pal. That's all.

MATT: *(Cooly.)* And I'd love to help with that but, as I've said about a gazillion times, I haven't seen or heard from Jane at all.

Pause.

WILL: Of course. Sorry. I'll…see you at dinner.

MATT: Yep.

WILL *exits.*

Silence.

MATT *listens out for **WILL**'s footsteps. Furtively gets up. Reaches under his bed. Takes out a poster of Jane Fonda as Barbarella. Kisses the poster somewhat solemnly and chastely.*

MATT: You and me are gonna have to be more careful, Jane. I think he's onto us.

LOVE BITE #6

The Hermitage. A big oak tree. 12:53 pm.

A big oak tree.

OLIVER *is pissing on the tree.*

A bottle of cider is perched in the roots.

OLIVER: It's me again.
You don't mind, do you?
You're a tree so it's probably good for you.
So what's new with you? Chloroplasts all in order? I must say you're looking wonderfully deciduous today.

Pause.
You going to ask me how I'm getting on?
No?
Well, I…
I, my fine leafy friend, have got… a girlfriend!

Pause.
What do you think of that then?

Beat.
Yeah I was surprised too.

Beat.
Now don't be looking at me like that.
She's a girl and you're a tree.
Completely different.
So no need to be rustling your branches all jealous, likes.

I met her at Judo.
Did I mention I do Judo now?
I do Judo now.
For like…self-defence and stuff.

And because Mum said I needed to do something to get me out of the house and keep my mind off things.

Meet new people.

Stuff like that.

He sits in the roots.
Pours a little cider into the ground

Cheers.

He takes a swig.

I'd have brought her to meet you but I don't think she'd understand.
Plus I don't think she'd approve of your constant drinking.

He pours some more cider for the tree.
Shame …you'd like her.

Pause.
In fact no you wouldn't.
You'd say she was crap.

He thinks for a bit.
Is she crap?
I don't think she's crap.

Pause.
Maybe a bit crap.
She's not as much fun as you.

*An acorn falls into **OLIVER**'s lap.*
Is this for me?

Pause.
Why would I want that?
I'm not a squirrel or a pig or something.
Acorns are poisonous to humans.
If I ate loads of acorns I'd get really sick and then my organs would shut down and then…

Pause.
You can be a real arsehole sometimes.

Silence.

Did you mean it? *(Pause.)* I saw your Mum the other day and she thinks you didn't but...did you?
 I promise I won't tell anyone.

Laughs.
I was just thinking about the 'extreme cider challenge'.
Remember?
When you bet me you could tan an entire two litre bottle of 'Frosty Jack's' in a oner?
I was all like 'you'll be sick, man' and you were all like 'No,no'.

Laughs.
'No, no.' you were like.
And then I'm rubbing your back and you're spewing all over the golf links but you're laughing as well, and the more you laugh the more you spew.
And then I can't stop laughing, and I laugh so hard that I start being sick too.
So we're both rolling about the place in a hysterical fit of the voms and Becky Knowles comes over and she's all like 'Youse are mingin!' and you just turn to her with cider puke all over your chin and go 'Aye, but you're boring'.

Laughs.

'Aye, but you're boring'
You couldn't cope with things being boring, could ya?

Pause.
That's probably what you'd say to my girlfriend.
She'd be like 'You're a tree' and you'd be like 'Aye but you're boring'
What's it like?
Being a tree?
Is being a tree boring?
Maybe I should become a tree too.
Then maybe all our particles and atoms and dust and stuff could all become a part of the same tree and we could grow and sway and photosynthesise together as the same big thing.

This thought upsets him.

And then nothing would be boring, or exciting, or good, or bad, or frightening, or sad, or lonely ever again because I'd just be a tree.

Holds up the acorn.
Fuck it.

Okay then.

OLIVER *tries to eat the acorn.*

It is disgusting but he keeps trying.

Eventually **OLIVER** *dry bokes and spits it out.*

Bleeeeurgh! Bloody hell mate!

He gargles with cider and spits.

He sits.

He looks up at the tree.

You're not here though, are you?

He touches the tree.

The little bits that made you up are.
But you're not.
I forgive you
And I miss you
And I love you
Don't you fuckin laugh ya---

Dummy punches at the tree...

Sighs.

He pours the cider slowly into the roots.

Same time tomorrow then.

He exits.

LOVE BITE #7

Princes Street Gardens. A bench. 12:59 pm.

SHY BOY *and* **PHONE GIRL** *sit next to each other on the bench.* **PHONE GIRL** *is still deeply engrossed in texting.* **SHY BOY** *sits stealing glances at* **PHONE GIRL**.

He glances then shuffles himself along the bench so he's closer to her.

Pause.

He glances again and shuffles.

Pause.

He glances again, hesitates, then moves right up next to her.

PHONE GIRL *continues to ignore him.*

Long pause.

SHY BOY *attempts a 'yawn and hug' style manoeuvre.*

The 'One o'clock gun' goes off.

SHY BOY *shrieks and jumps.*

PHONE GIRL *doesn't react.*

SHY BOY: One o'clock already. Wow.

 Sound of pigeons. **SHY BOY** *looks around.*

SHY BOY: Aren't pigeons cool!

 PHONE GIRL *slowly turns round and gives* **SHY BOY** *a 'look'.*

SHY BOY: Actually no. Pigeons are crap. I hate pigeons. Piss off you scabby disease-ridden pigeons you!

 Kicks out at the pigeons.

PHONE GIRL *continues to give* **SHY BOY** *a 'look'.*

Pause.

SHY BOY: Actually I'm kinda ambivalent about pigeons.

PHONE GIRL *goes back to her texting.*

Silence.

SHY BOY: I really like hanging out with you.

LOVE BITE #8

The playground. 1:05pm

REMY *and* **LEO**.

LEO: Whatcha got there, Remy?

REMY: A very not dangerous and not tellable-onable game.

LEO: Right. A boring game.

REMY: No. An actually very fun game actually. Made it up just now.

LEO: Kay.

REMY: It's called Happy Clapping.

LEO: That is a good name.

REMY: Thanks. The way you play it see, is one of us throws this very not dangerous acorn in the air.

LEO: Go on.

REMY: And the other one of us has to bet on how many times they can clap before it hits the ground.

LEO: Hits the ground.

REMY: Yes. And if the clapper wins, they get to keep the acorn. And then it's their turn. But if the clapper loses…then the acorn guy…

LEO: I'm listening.

REMY: The acorn guy gets to kick the clapper.

Beat.
What do you think?

LEO: I think you're amazing and that's the best game ever and I love you. Okay let's do it…

ELLIE *enters.*

ELLIE: Can I play?

LEO: Play what, Ellie? Not playing anything. We're not…like…like *playas*.

ELLIE: Lying's naughty, Leo. I heard you. You're playing Happy Clapping.

LEO: That's not even a thing. Is it, Remy?

REMY: Uh…

LEO: Remy?

REMY: *(Hushed.)* Lying's naughty, Leo.

ELLIE: Pleeease can I play. Pleeease. No one ever lets me play anything.

LEO: Oh and I wonder why that is? *(Beat.)* It's because you're a big tell-tale-booobie. That's why.

ELLIE: Not one.

LEO: You are and you know it!

REMY: Leo…

ELLIE: Well if you think I'm a big tell-tale boobie, maybe I should just go be a tell-tale boobie. If that's what you think.

LEO: How? We've not done anything wrong.

ELLIE: I heard the rules. Kicking! Kicking's definitely naughty.

REMY: No…no we didn't say kicking it was…uh…kissing. If you lose the bet you get a good hard….kiss.

ELLIE: Oh. *(Blushes.)* Please may I play?

LEO: No, Ellie. No you mayn't.

Beat.

ELLIE: Acorns are poisonous to people. If one fell in yer mouth. MRS PHILLIPS!!!

REMY: OKAY! Okay you can play just…shhh.

ELLIE *squeeees in delight.*

ELLIE: YAAAY! Wait a minute though. We need two teams for this. Boys against girls.

REMY: Uh…okay…

ELLIE: GRACE! Grace come over here. We're all of us gunna play a game.

> **GRACE** *enters.* **REMY** *doesn't know what to do with himself.*

GRACE: Hi Remy.

> **REMY** *tries to say hi but makes a little 'Eeep' noise instead.*

ELLIE: Did you hear the rules, Grace?

GRACE: No.

ELLIE: Well, you'll pick it up. SO! Grace and Remy go first. Then it's me and Leo's turn. *(Giggles.)*

> **LEO** *makes a disgusted noise.*

ELLIE: This is gonna be so much fun! Remy, how many claps do you bet?

REMY: Uh…uh one?

ELLIE: Five? Five.

REMY: No I said…

ELLIE: Five it is. Now Grace. Throw this acorn as high as you can in the air. Ready Remy?

REMY: Ooh.

ELLIE: Three, two, one…throw!

> **REMY** *claps.*

ELLIE/LEO: One! Two! Three! Four!…

> *On the fifth clap* **REMY** *claps* **GRACE** *in the face.* **GRACE** *lets out a cry and storms off.*
>
> *Pause.*

ELLIE: MRS PHILLIPS!!

She exits.

LEO: WHY REMY? WHY??

REMY: I DON'T KNOW!!!

LOVE BITE #9

SFX: A school yard fight. 1:10PM Pupils chanting and goading the fighters on. The sound of an impact, loud OOH!. The sound of the crowd dispersing.

SHELLY *enters at a swift walk.*

SADIE: *(Offstage.)* Whoooo! That's what you get ya wee skank.

> **SHELLY** *pauses momentarily.*

SADIE: Shelly!

> **SHELLY** *continues to walk.*

SADIE: SHELLY!

> **SADIE** *enters at jog. She has a slight bruise above her eye.*

SHELLY: Hiya Sadie.

SADIE: Can you believe that…? Ahm no bein funny but. Can you actually believe?

SHELLY: Yeah. Rough.

SADIE: I'll say. No need tae thank us. Trash talkin wee wank.

> **SHELLY** *nods.*

SADIE: Like I said, no need to thank us. I mean, who does she think she is?

> *Pushes* **SHELLY** *jovially.*
>
> *Shelly doesn't respond.*

SADIE: Tragic. Tragic seeing people like that…it's pure desperate, eh?

SHELLY: Aye. Desperate.

SADIE: No need to thank us.

> **SHELLY** *smiles weakly and nods.*
>
> *Awkward beat.*

SADIE: You saw it though? Tell me you saw it.

SHELLY: Well no. I was in the library so…

SADIE: Oh right. The Library, aye?

SHELLY: Aye.

SADIE: Hiding?

SHELLY: Reading.

SADIE: Hiding. I don't blame ya. She's a pure unit, man.

SHELLY: I think Emily…I think she has.. like weight issues….probably linked to…

SADIE: Pies.

SHELLY: …diabetes.

SADIE: Even still. No excuse for lashing out. I mean, like, we've all got problems, mate.

SHELLY: Yeah but – and I'm not trying to be ungrateful here – but was all of that really necessary?

SADIE: Was all of what really necessary?

SHELLY: Just…what I heard…

SADIE: What you heard from the library? *(Beat.)* Look, she called you an anorexic wee bitch, mate. Said she was gonna kick yer head in just for interrupting her in English.

SHELLY: Allegedly.

SADIE: What?

SHELLY: Nothing. No, I'm grateful for you sticking up for me but…

SADIE: But what?

SHELLY: Nothing

SADIE: No. But what?

SHELLY: Just… the face scratching? I mean, she was already on the ground. So was there really any need –

SADIE: So you did see it?

SHELLY:….

SADIE: What's with you saying you didn't then? *(Laughs.)* Like, what's that all about?

SHELLY: I'm sorry, pal. I really need to be shooting off.

SADIE: Sound. Where we going?

SHELLY: Uh, well I was going…

SADIE: Not hanging out with those LARPING fannies again are ya?

SHELLY: They're my friends.

SADIE: Aye, yer pals. New wee pally-wallies, that's sound. No offence, I'm sure some of them are cool. But even still, I've known ya the longest so…

SHELLY: I didn't know it was a competition.

SADIE: Competition? Nahnah I'm not saying that. I'm not saying that. Just sayin. Us two. Tight since play-group. That's all I'm sayin.

SHELLY *nods.*

Awkward pause.

SADIE: I'm guessing I'm not invited if it's the LARPING fannies, eh?

SHELLY: Sadie…

SADIE: No hassle… If people want to skip about the links all day dressed like Gandalf that's up to them, no judgement here. It's not for me is all I'm saying. So zero fudges are given if you're not inviting me. *(Beat.)* That's where you're off to though, isn't it?

SHELLY: I'm just going to the cinema, pal.

SADIE: Aw well in that case, no excuse! That plan can just get itself right in the sea!

SHELLY: Sorry?

SADIE: Here's what we're gonna do. We're gonna nash back to yours. Get some frickin Dominos in and then watch some MMA.

SHELLY: MMA's pay per view

SADIE: Well we'll use yer brother's login. He's got a PayPal account

SHELLY: He works at Forbidden Planet. He can't afford…

SADIE: If he can afford a bespoke 'Valerian steel' sword like all those LARPING fannies, he can afford a measly pay-per view, surely!

SHELLY: Maybe but…

SADIE: *(Mimicking.)* Maybe but but…

SHELLY: It's just…

SADIE: It's just…it's just what?

SHELLY: – I don't want to, right? I don't want to.

Pause.

SADIE: But… you have to.

SHELLY: I have to?

SADIE: Well no, you don't – what I'm saying is…Seriously, what's wrong with you today?

SHELLY: There's nothing wrong with me.

Beat.

SADIE: What's that supposed to mean?

SHELLY: Nothing.

SADIE: Nono. If you've got something to say. Just say it.

SHELLY: I'm just…tired, pal. Okay? I just want to go home.

Silence.

SADIE: Fine.

SHELLY: Sorry.

SADIE: It's fine.

Awkward pause.

SHELLY *starts to walk away.*

SADIE: Maybe I should just leave you to fight your own battles in future. Maybe next time someone says they're gonna batter you after-school I'll just not bother my arse, eh?

SHELLY: Next time. Right.

SADIE: What do you mean by that?

SHELLY: What really happened with Emily, pal?

SADIE: What you talking about?

SHELLY: Y'know what? Nothing.

SADIE: Nono. Not nothing.

SADIE *blocks* **SHELLY**'s *path*

You sayin I made it up? Emily sayin she was gonna batter you? Is that what you're saying?

SHELLY: *(Shrugs.)*

SADIE: Think I'd make up something like that just to get you to hang out with me? Think I'd take a slap for that? Get over yourself, pal.

SHELLY: You didn't take a slap though. I mean, I didn't see –

SADIE: *(Pointing to her injured face.)* WHAT DO YA CALL THAT THEN!

SHELLY: *(Shaken.)* Okay. You're being aggressive now.

SADIE: I'M NOT BEING AGGRESSIVE!

SHELLY: *(Walking away.)* Okay. Bye Sadie.

SADIE: Fine! Not even bothered! Plenty of other mates I could be hanging out with!

SHELLY: *(Under her breath.)* Imaginary mates.

SADIE: What?

    SHELLY *blocks* **SADIE**'s *path.*

SADIE: Go and say that to my face then.

SHELLY: Let me past, Sadie.

SADIE: Nup. Go and say it to my face.

SHELLY: Let me past.

SADIE: Say it!

    Beat. **SHELLY** *has had enough.*

SHELLY: Alright. I said imaginary pals. As in 'what pals'. As in, 'seriously, what pals do you even have, pal.' There.

    Beat.

SADIE: Take that back.

SHELLY: No.

SADIE: Take it back. Now.

SHELLY: I mean who'd want to be pals with such a massive…

SADIE: What?

    Shoves her.

SADIE: Such a massive what?!

SHELLY: Bully!

    SADIE *punchs* **SHELLY**. *Is shocked by her own actions.*

SADIE: Sorry,

    SHELLY *touches her lip.*

    There is blood.

    She stares at **SADIE**.

    Starts to quietly chuckle.
I'm sorry.

SHELLY *slowly and self-assuredly, exits.*

C'mon.

Shelly, please…

I said I was sorry

WHAT'S YER FRICKIN PROBLEM, PAL?!

SADIE *is now alone.*

She repeatedly strikes and scratches herself in the face

LOVE BITE #10

1.45 **PM**. **COLLETE** *and* **JOE** *stand facing the audience. When they speak it is as if they are rehearsing what they plan to say in front of a mirror.*

COLLETTE: Joe, I dunno how best to put this but…I think you are awesome.

JOE: Collette. I think you're great. Like, really really…uh, good.

COLLETTE: Actually awesome's probably the wrong word. Awesome kinda implies something huge and, like, dizzyingly terrifying. Like the Grand Canyon.

JOE: Well, maybe great's a bit –. I think you're…above average? No.

COLLETTE: So, not awesome. You Joe are… AMAZEBALLS.

JOE: Collette, I've always found you… fair to middling? Not terrible? No you can't say that, Joe. You're… fine, Collette. I think you're fine.

COLLETTE: Totes amazeballs the best boyfriend ever. Though I'm sure you don't need me to tell you that. Cos it always seemed like your self-esteem was…like, uh, pretty high. Which is a good thing really!

JOE: And so, our time like kinda seeing each other. Well, it's been real. No Joe that makes you sound like a complete douchebag. It's been… Nice. You're a really nice person, Collette. Which makes what I have to say now…kinda more difficult than it should be…

COLLETTE: But, y'know, people can surprise you, can't they? Cos I'm gonna be truthful, Joe. The first time I met you…on your way back from the playing fields with the rest of the under-18s team, like all covered in mud and spitting in the hedges and calling everyone a 'gaylord'…well, kinda I guessed you must be a bit of a douchebag. And I don't know, maybe you didn't realise at the time or just didn't care, but you got a bit of spit in my friend Abby's hair. As you walked past. Didn't look at us or acknowledge what you'd done or anything. And Abby said, I'm not sure if she was joking a bit or what, but Abby said, 'I'm never washing my hair again'. 'Spose you're used to having that effect on people though, eh. Haha! but…that's a bit sad making isn't it? Knowing that people like you cos of how you look…

JOE: But, Collette, this can't be too much of a shock to you really. Cos you're lovely but, like, you don't exactly look after yourself, do you? Always wearing those massive jumpers. And I've seen you with make-up on before… Mind I bought you a bunch o' stuff from Superdrug before that Under the Sea ball? And done up, I'm being serious Collette, you looked a solid 7…I mean, you looked great! 'Cept you were that quiet and awkward with it on. Anyway, it's not like I care about all that. Cos, honestly, I really don't. It's just…you know what people our age are like. Shallow bunch of pricks. Still, you'd have bin saving yourself and…and me, like, a lot of grief if you could've just learnt to…to make a wee bit of an effort y'know?

COLLETTE: But don't worry, Joe. I honestly don't care about stuff like that. The reason I liked you Joe is…well, do you remember? You'll probably be all embarrassed but… remember that party for Oliver's friend Jamie? The one who died. Our whole year group was there. And everyone was really drunk. All hugging and saying how much they loved each other. But you were nowhere to be seen. And it was completely by accident that I found you. Just sitting, in the garden, by yourself. And…it might have been cos it was all dark and rainy, but, your face. It looked like you had been crying. And when I asked if you were sad about Jamie you said yes but…that wasn't the reason. And then you said that you hated rugby. And that no one understood that it was all about appearances. And that you sometimes wished…. Then, I remember, you asked if it would be alright if you had a hug. Not in a creepy way. In a sad way. And I said of course, Joe, of course you can have a hug. And that's when I started liking you, Joe. Only then. Because you're not a douche. You're just… a silly boy, Joe.

JOE: And another thing, Colette, the talking. I mean, sure, it's good to talk but…there's a limit. You always want to know how I feel about stuff. Look, I understand it's important to vent from time to time. But see… talking about your feelings too much, Colette well…it makes you weak.

Yeah. It just makes you weak.

So. Taking into account all of what I've just said…I think it would be best…

COLETTE: …A silly boy. And that's okay. I understand. It must be difficult. I'm sure you'll work it out. But…I'm sorry, Joe. It's a problem I can't take on anymore. I can't allow that to be my problem. I hope you understand. So, I don't know how to put this exactly, but I think it would be best…for both of us…

JOE: If we didn't see each other anymore.

COLETTE: If we…just became friends.

JOE/COLETTE: I hope you understand.

Blackout.

COLLETTE *and* **JOE** *at school the next day.*

COLLETTE: Hello you.

JOE: Hi, Colette. Listen…

COLLETTE: Give us a squeeze

She hugs **JOE**. **JOE** *hugs back awkwardly.*

COLLETTE: *(Gently.)* Joe. I was wondering if we could maybe…

JOE: We need to talk.

COLLETTE: Oh. Okay. Cool. Of course. You go…first.

JOE: Listen Colette. I'm not sure how to put this…but I've been doing a lot of thinking and…

COLLETTE: Yeah?

JOE: I think…it would be best…if we stopped seeing each other.

COLLETTE: Oh! *(She laughs slightly.)*

JOE: I hope you understand.

COLLETTE: Oh no totally! Totally I understand. I agree, in fact.

JOE: Sorry?

COLLETTE: I agree. I think that would totally be the best for thing for both of us. In fact, that's what I was going to talk to you about.

JOE: *(Trying to hide his crestfallenness.)* Oh. You were?

COLLETTE: Totally! Haha! What a relief.

JOE: Yeah. A….relief. Yeah.

Beat
So. You're not sad then?

COLLETTE: No! Well, of course I'm a bit sad. But it wasn't really working was it?

JOE: I…no. I guess it wasn't, no.

COLLETTE: Are… you sad?

JOE: Me? No! Nono. I'm grand, pal.

COLLETTE: That's good. I wouldn't want you to be sad, Joe.

Silence.

COLLETTE: Well, I guess this is…actually let's not say goodbye cos that's a bit, y'know, 'boohoohoo'.

JOE: Yeah, it's…

COLLETTE *hugs* **JOE** *and kisses him on the cheek.*

COLLETTE: You're a great guy, Joe. I'll miss ya. Stay in touch.

JOE: Yeah,…I'll…
Miss you too.

COLLETTE *goes to exit.*

JOE: Colette…?

COLETTE: Yes Joe?

JOE: Nothing, I guess. Nothing.

COLLETTE *exits.*

JOE *stands in silence.*

Lights slowly fade.

The bench, **CUPID** *and* **MALCOLM**.

MALCOLM: Aw mate, all a tad depressing.

CUPID: Frame it how you want, matey.

MALCOLM: How are the wee yins getting on? Have they got the hang of it yet?

CUPID: Hmm. Depends on how you look at it 'spose.

LOVE BITE #11

2.45pm The playground.

GRACE *and* **ELLIE** *are playing with Barbies.*

LEO *enters purposefully,* **REMY** *follows.*

REMY: Oh Leo dooon't

LEO: Hi Ellie! Hi Grace!

BOTH: Hi Leo.

LEO: What you got there? Barbies?

BOTH: Yup.

LEO: Oh. Oh no.

ELLIE: What?

LEO: Dunno if you know 'n stuff but like…Barbies aren't allowed in the playground anymore. Barbies aren't allowed in the playground anymore are they, Remy?

REMY: Ken.

LEO: *(Beat.)* Haha. That's…you're funny. But serious. Not allowed.

ELLIE: How come?

LEO: Choking hazard. Mrs Phillips said no to them.

ELLIE: Yeah?

LEO: Yeah. Cos I went and said to her 'Mrs Phillips they're a choking hazard'. How do you like them apples?!

ELLIE: Choking hazard?? Huh. Maybe the way you play with them.

LEO: Whatever. I don't make the rules. You made your bed and there is a lion in it. Hand over the Barbies.

They ignore **LEO**.

LEO: Mrs Phillips! MRS PHILLIPS!

ELLIE *stares at* **LEO**. *Laughs.*

LEO: OH! So it's okay for you to play with Barbies and not us? It's okay for you to ruin our fun but when we do the same thing…

That. is. Very. Unfair.

Pause.

ELLIE *stares at* **LEO** *and* **REMY**.

Starts to laugh even harder.

LEO: Why is she laughing??!

REMY: I don't know but… let's go.

LEO: Hand over the Barbie, Ellie.

ELLIE: Not gunna.

LEO: Gimme the Barbie! It's not fair!

ELLIE: Nup!

LEO *pushes* **ELLIE** *over*

Shocked silence.

ELLIE *gets up.*

LEO: Ellie. I'm sorry.

ELLIE *looks strangely pleased. She giggles. Hands him the Barbie. Pecks him on the cheek. Exits.*

LEO: I…uh…I…

    LEO *exits leaving* **GRACE** *and* **REMY**.

REMY: Dunno what that was all about.

GRACE: Hm.
Okay.
Remy?

REMY: Yeah?

    GRACE *pushes* **REMY** *over.*

REMY: OWWW! THAT REALLY HUUURT!

GRACE: Yeah. It does, doesn't it?

Love Bite #12

1.30pm Matt's room.

MATT *is in pyjamas talking to the 'Jane Fonda'.*

MATT: What's that Jane?

> *Beat.*
> Why thank you, yes, they are nice pyjamas.
> Star Wars
> My mum got me them
> For Christmas
>
> *Beat.*
> Oh stop it you

> **WILL** *suddenly burst in.*
> Don't come in! I'm naked!

MATT *chucks a cover over* **JANE**.

WILL: You're. Not. Naked!
> Who you talkin to? Huh?

MATT: No one.

WILL: I heard talking.

MATT: I was…practising lines. For the school production of…

WILL: Barbarella?

MATT: I have no idea what that word means.

WILL: Suuuuuure.

> **WILL** *scans the room suspiciously. Sits on the bed.*

MATT: Don't. Don't sit there, you'll crumple…

WILL: I'll what?

MATT: You'll crumple…my bed. With your big… arse, you'll crumple it right in on itself. Look, have you ever heard of knocking?

WILL: Forget knocking. Have you ever heard of…Betrayal??

***WILL** whips the covers back to reveal **JANE**.*

Beat.

*Both brothers dive for **JANE**.*

MATT: Let her go! You'll hurt her!

WILL: She's mine!

MATT: You said she doesn't belong to anyone! And that…you'd understand cos you were my brother and…!

WILL: It's called coaxing a confession, ya backstabbing lil rat-faced twat! Now un-hand her!

MATT: No! She can't go back to you! Not the way you treat her!

WILL: Get yer own, Jane!

MATT: SHAN'T!

The poster rips in two.

Horrified pause.

BOTH: What have you done??!

LOVE BITE #13

Princes Street Gardens. A bench. 3:06pm.

SHY BOY *and* **PHONE GIRL** *sit next to each other on the bench.* **SHY BOY** *is holding an ice cream with a flake. He holds it out expectantly to* **SHY GIRL**. *She ignores him and continues to text. He offers it again. She ignores him. Pause.* **SHY BOY** *laughs loudly and falsely.*

SHY BOY: Hahaha! I am…I am such a…such a doofus, right. Went and bought this ice-cream and then thought, like, 'What am I doing! I can't eat this! I'm lactose intolerant!' How daft is that? Then I thought maybe you'd…you'd…

Silence.

SHY BOY: It's got a flake in it.

Silence.

SHY BOY: Only one pound seventy.

Silence.

SHY BOY: Like my bus fare.

Silence.

SHY BOY *carefully places the ice cream on a napkin and carefully places it on the bench next to* **PHONE GIRL**.

Silence.

He gets up to leave.

Without looking at him **PHONE GIRL** *grabs* **SHY BOY**'s *thigh and gives it a squeeze.*

SHY BOY *makes a little 'peeping' noise of terror and elation and sits back down.*

LOVE BITE #14

3:25pm. James Gillespies High School. The wall by the car park.

MARK *is sitting on the wall.* **QUENTIN** *is pacing back and forth restlessly.*

MARK *watches him for a while amused.*

MARK: Ha.

>   **QUENTIN** *stops and gives* **MARK** *a look of intense stress.*

QUENTIN: What do you mean by 'Ha'? What's 'Ha' supposed to mean?

MARK: Nothing. Just 'Ha' is all.

QUENTIN: People don't just 'Ha' for no reason. What's with the 'Ha'?

MARK: Jeez Quentin. It was just a little 'Ha'. No need to get all 'up in my shit' about it.

QUENTIN: The last thing I want is to be up in anyone's shit…but… c'mon…at least tell me what kind of a 'Ha' it was. I mean was it an "I just remembered how Stuart got caught doodling a swastika in his vocab jotter in double German this morning. Wasn't that funny? I'm going to go 'Ha' now" sort of 'Ha'? Or was is a 'Ha' of sudden realisation, as if you're thinking something like "If I get a Snickers from the tuck shop rather than from Margie's I'll have one pound twenty left…hang on…that's enough for a half pizza and chips! Ha!". Or was it a "Look at Quentin. Look at pimply ol Quentin with his unfortunate eyebrows and his worriesome face. Isn't Quentin a dickhead? Yes. Yes he is. HA."

MARK: If you must know it was a benign 'Ha' of mild amusement.

QUENTIN: Oh. A benign 'Ha' of mild amusement was it? Great. I'm glad my inner torment is only slightly funny to you.

MARK: Sorry mate. It's just the pacing. I didn't think anyone actually paced up and down in real life.

QUENTIN: Look, I'm trying to make a very difficult decision here and you're really not helping.

MARK: To be fair it's not that difficult a decision. Either you ask her and you maybe go or you don't ask her and you don't go. Now, judging by the way you go on about her all the time and check her Instagram at least twice a day and go all giggling and twitchy when she pays you the least bit of attention I'm guessing you probably do want to go with her. Therefore it makes logical sense for you to pick the option most likely to yield this result i.e. asking her.

QUENTIN: Logic has nothing to do with it.

MARK: Do you want her to go to this Leavers disco, prom, ball, hootenanny, shindig, hingummy with you or not?

QUENTIN: Yes. Yes I do. More than anyone has ever wanted anything in the world ever.

MARK: Okay…fine… Why exactly? She's gonna be there anyway. Besides, if you've got a lassie in tow there's no way you'll be able to go tanning big beastie behind the bins with me.

QUENTIN: I know…I know…but still.

MARK: Why?

QUENTIN: Because…Because it's Ashley Hannigan is why.

MARK: Um…yeah. I know it's Ashley Hannigan. What? That completely didn't answer my question.

QUENTIN: She's…she's amazing though.

MARK: At what?

QUENTIN: No…No she's just generally amazing.

MARK: She's crap at ping-pong. I whooped her ass at ping-pong.

QUENTIN: No you don't understand. It's just the way she kinda nibbles the end of her pencil in class and leans back in her chair so that there's only one leg left on the floor, and the way that she always says things are 'ace!' even when they're clearly not 'ace!' and the way that she always does her lip salve when she's talking to you but never ever breaks eye contact.

Pause.

MARK: And that's amazing is it?

QUENTIN: Yes.

MARK: Well then. It's a no brainer isn't it? Just go up to her and ask her if she wants to go to the dance with you. Easy-peasy-poo.

QUENTIN: It's not easy-peasy-poo. It's the least easy-peasy-poo thing I can think of.

MARK:. It's the easyiest-peasiest-poosiest thing in the world. I mean come on! What's the worst that can happen?

QUENTIN: I don't want to answer that question. It's a terrible question. Let's avoid that question altogether thank you very much.

MARK: The worst thing that can happen is that she says no.

Pause.

QUENTIN: You think you're so helpful don't you? I know that's the worst thing that could happen.

MARK: Well, doesn't that make you feel better?

QUENTIN: No!

MARK: Oh…Okay…why?

QUENTIN: Because her saying 'no' therefore making it obvious that she doesn't like me in 'that' way is probably the single most painful thing that I could imagine happening to me.

MARK: Even more painful than being kicked in the balls?

QUENTIN: Much more painful.

MARK: Even a kick in the balls where it just clips one of them and you feel like you're gonna be sick for like twenty minutes afterwards?

QUENTIN: Yes.

MARK: Jesus.

Pause.

MARK: If you asked her…and she said no…I'm sure she wouldn't be mean about it. I don't think Ashley's amazing…but she's cool…she'd definitely not be a dick about it.

QUENTIN: I know she wouldn't be but…thing is…right now when I see her nibbling her pencil or saying something's 'Ace!' when it's actually quite shit, or doing her lip salve whilst talking, I just feel really, really happy, y'know? And I know that if I tell her…if she finds out that I think she's amazing…and she doesn't think I'm even a little bit amazing back…I know the next time I see her nibbling her pencil I'll just feel sad. Really really sad. And I don't want to see her nibbling her pencil and feel sad. I really don't.

Pause.

MARK: Maybe you should just tell her you think she's amazing.

QUENTIN: You think? You think that would be a good idea?

MARK: Who knows eh? Sounds like the kinda pish girls like but if she KB's ya there's plenty mair fish in the sea!

QUENTIN: You were so close to being helpful there…so close.

MARK: So what's the plan Stan? She's gonna be out of her Euphonium lesson any minute now. What you gonna do?

QUENTIN: I'm gonna pace up and down some more.

MARK: Nut. I mean in regards to…y'know…

QUENTIN: I'm gonna…gonna…I'll probably just leave it.

MARK: Probably just leave it.

QUENTIN: Aye.

MARK: Then what? Go home?

QUENTIN: Aye.

MARK: Fair enough.

Silence.

MARK: Actually no. Not fair enough at all.

QUENTIN: What?

MARK: It's all about you isn't it?

QUENTIN opens his mouth to speak.

MARK: I would love for someone to tell me they think I'm amazing. Even if it was like…Bridget Vallance from Class 7 that told me. Y'know, the one with slushy 'S's and the retainer and the blanket acne. It would still make me feel awesome. And you're gonna deprive Ashley of that just cos you might end up feeling bad? That's lame man.

QUENTIN: Lame?

MARK: Lame as a no-legged Christmas orphan lying crutchless in the snow.

QUENTIN: That lame?

MARK: Lamer.

QUENTIN: Alright then I'll tell her! I'll tell her right to her big smelly face! Then we'll see who's lame!

MARK: So you're gonna tell her?

QUENTIN: Aye. Yeah. Totally.

MARK: Good cos that's her just coming out of Warrender now.

QUENTIN looks panicked.

QUENTIN: Actually I might just phone her…or text her… or something…

MARK: You don't have her number.

QUENTIN: Right…yeah…I'll write it in her homework diary…I sit next to her in Geography…sometimes.

MARK: OR!…you could just tell her now.

QUENTIN: I'll get her on Snapchat.

MARK: Frickin… Snapchat?! Look, If you're not gonna go through with it just go man. Just leave.

QUENTIN: I will. I'll do it…I'll…oh…

QUENTIN *legs it.*

ASHLEY *enters carrying her Euphonium in a bin bag.*

ASHLEY: Why's Quentin running away?

MARK: He's not.

ASHLEY: It looks like it. I haven't done anything wrong have I?

MARK: Nah. He's got a bladder problem. Coward's urethra they call it. Can kick in at any time apparently.

ASHLEY: Poor Quentin. Was gonna show him how I'd learnt to play the Rocky theme tune. The Rocky theme tune's ace! Quentin likes the Rocky theme tune I think…He always hums it in P.E when he's getting geared up to climb up the gym ropes.

MARK: You can play the Rocky theme on that?

ASHLEY: Yep. Pretty ace huh?

MARK: Go on then. Give us a blast.

ASHLEY: Um…well…I've only just learnt it so…

MARK: Come on. Rocky it up.

ASHLEY: 'kay.

She takes out the Euphonium and makes a few feeble 'oompah' noises.

MARK: Ha.

ASHLEY: Ha? What's 'Ha' supposed to mean?

MARK: Nothing. Just didn't realise it was an 'oompah' band instrument. Y'know like 'OOMPAH OOMPAH OOMPAH!'. Like a big lame-o 'oompah' band, y'know.

ASHLEY: Oh.

Pause.

MARK: Oompah.

ASHLEY: It was shit, wasn't it?

MARK: What? No! No no no. I mean…it was just…it was just…oompah.

ASHLEY: It was shit. I'm shit at everything. Can't do Euphonium, can't do 'Ping Pong'…

MARK: Ha! Yeah you can't! Sorry.

ASHLEY: Can't do anything…

MARK: Well…y'know…Practise makes perfect.

ASHLEY: I guess…yeah…yeah you're right…thanks Mark.

Goes to leave.

MARK: Ashley?

ASHLEY: Uh-huh.

MARK: Someone thinks you're amazing by the way.

ASHLEY: Oh. Okay. Amazing at what?

MARK: Not at stuff…well some stuff…weird stuff like chairs and lip salve and eye-contact and nibbling and…

ASHLEY: Euphonium?

MARK: No.

ASHLEY: Oh.

MARK: Well…probably Euphonium…everything really…they just think you're amazing…in general.

ASHLEY: Really?

MARK: Really.

ASHLEY: Wow. That's…

MARK: Ace?

ASHLEY *nods enthusiastically.*

MARK: Yeah. It is, isn't it.

MALCOLM *snaps out of the trance.*

MALCOLM: Whoa.

CUPID: Now do you see what I mean? Now do you see why you humans are impossible to work with?

MALCOLM: Um…well…

CUPID: What do you mean um well? It's all a massive dysfunctional shit show. I don't even know why I bother sometimes.

MALCOLM: But it wasn't all bad. Some of it was kinda…I dunno. Kinda beautiful.

CUPID: That's another thing I don't understand about youse fannies. Always seeming to think things are the most poignant when they go tits up.

MALCOLM: Well show me something where it doesn't go tits up then.

CUPID: It always goes tits up in one way or another.

MALCOLM: Come on. I'm sure it's not all bad.

CUPID: Hmmph.

LOVE BITE #15

3.51pm. **GEORGE** *is sitting centre stage eating from a huge tub of ice-cream.*

His phone rings.

He ignores it.

His phone rings again.

He lets out a slightly theatrical sigh. Answers it.

GEORGE: Yello?

CHLOE: *Screams of anguish*

GEORGE: Oh hi, Chloe.

CHLOE: Hi, George. You busy?

GEORGE: Yes. Very

CHLOE: How busy we talkin?

GEORGE: Well, I'm on my second tub of Ben and Jerry's and I'm about two thirds of the way through 'The Notebook' so…yeah. *(Beat.)* You up to much?

CHLOE: Not much. Probably just gonna go kill everyone, y'know?

GEORGE: Oh. Cool. *(Beat.)* Everyone?

CHLOE: Yeah. With a big knife. Starting with 'HER' then myself and then EVERYONE.

GEORGE: So the whole you guys meeting for coffee and a 'let's just be friends' chat went well then, I take it?

CHLOE: You could say that. *(Beat.)* Anyways, I probably won't start killing everyone for another ten mins or so. Gotta… limber up and stuff. Just thought you might want to know.

GEORGE: *(Sighs.)* I'll be over in twenty. Twenty-five tops.

CHLOE: Well, that's great. But murder spree's gonna start in ten so…

GEORGE: I'm sad and in my jammies and full of ice-cream, Chloe!

Beat.

CHLOE: Fifteen, then.

GEORGE: Fine. Bye.

CHLOE: kayLoveyoubye.

Fourteen and a half-mins later.
Chloe's bedroom.
CHLOE *is listening to death metal holding a knife to her own throat somewhat histrionically.*
GEORGE *enters, still eating ice-cream.*

GEORGE: Hi Chloe.

CHLOE: Which one's the carotid artery?

GEORGE: Oh. It's the big pulsy one. *(Holds two fingers to his throat.)* There.

CHLOE: Thought so. Cheers. I'd stand back if I were you. Gonna be skooshy.

GEORGE: What happened to the killing EVERYONE part of the plan?

CHLOE: That was the plans ten mins ago. Things change, George. Nothing in this life is certain except that we all die alone.

GEORGE: True dat.

CHLOE: Okay. Here we go. Don't try and stop me now.

GEORGE: Wouldn't dream of it. *(Takes a spoonful of ice-cream.)* Uh, Chloe? Would you like some…

CHLOE: What chu sayin?

GEORGE: Nothing. Forget it.

CHLOE: Nono. Would I like some what?

GEORGE: I was gonna say would you like some ice-cream. But clearly you're a bit busy for that.

CHLOE: Clearly.

GEORGE: Bit too busy ending your futile existence to eat ice-cream, aren't you Chloe?

CHLOE: Correct-ah-mundo.

GEORGE: I'm sure Ben and Jerry's Karamel Sutra is the last thing on your mind.

CHLOE: What!? Karamel frickin Sutra?! *(Throws the knife down.)* Gimme!

GEORGE: Hm I dunno. You don't wanna be killing yourself on a full stomach. It's like swimming.

CHLOE: Gimme ice-cream now! Chloe demands ice-cream!

GEORGE: Changed my mind. Get your own break-up ice-cream.

CHLOE: NO!!! KARAMEL SUTRA ME UP, BIIIIIIIITCH! – sorry what?

Break-up, ice-cream?

GEORGE *nods.*

Oh. Oh George babes I'm so sorry. What happened?

GEORGE: Isn't that obvious? Got dumped.

CHLOE: Well, yeah. But deets, man.

GEORGE: Oh I don't wanna bore you. Like, you've got your own shit going on so…

CHLOE: Me? Naaaah. *(Looks at the knife.)* Well, kinda. But forget all that noise. You're my absolute favourite person so…if you wanna chat?

GEORGE: Rory said I was being too needy…and that..he needed some space…

CHLOE: What?! Rory can shut his stupid face! You're not needy!

GEORGE: I am a bit needy though, amn't I?

CHLOE: Literally everyone's a 'bit needy'. But Rory didn't need to put it like that! I mean, there's such a thing as tact. What a dick!

GEORGE: He's not a dick. And…he didn't put it like that exactly. But his txt heavily implied…

CHLOE: His TXT?!!!

GEORGE: It's not as bad as it sounds..

CHLOE: He dumped you by TXT?!!

GEORGE: No. Whatsapp actually…

   CHLOE *picks up knife.*

CHLOE: Right, change of plans. No-more of your self-piteous 'let's all kill ourselves' nonsense.

GEORGE: That was totally your idea!

CHLOE: Whatever. New plan is we kill RORY.

GEORGE: *(Trying not to laugh.)* Kill Rory?

CHLOE: Well, maybe not kill. We maim Rory.

GEORGE: *(Laughing.)* Go on.

CHLOE: Then we do something to Little Miss 'I Kissed A Girl and momentarily liked It'. Something heinous.

GEORGE: Haha! Heinous like what?

CHLOE: I dunno. Poo through her letterbox or something. To be honest I'm rapidly ceasing to care about 'HER'. I'm more angry on your behalf.

GEORGE: *(Laughing.)* Awww. Aren't you sweet.

CHLOE: The sweetest. So? What do you think of the new plan?

GEORGE: I love the new plan. The new plan makes me happy.

CHLOE: Knew it would.

GEORGE: But what are we seriously going to do to make us feel better? Like, in actual real life?

CHLOE: In actual real life?

GEORGE *nods.*

CHLOE *drops the knife.*

CHLOE: No idea.

Beat.

GEORGE: I've got a few ideas.

Blackout.

The following montage is set to Gloria Gaynor's: I Will Survive.

GEORGE and **CHLOE** *drink Lambrini.*

They pin up a picture of Chloe's ex's face.

Throw darts at it.

They all miss.

CHLOE *grabs the picture, tears holes through the eyes.*

GEORGE *watches, slightly perturbed.*

CHLOE *hold the picture up to her face like a mask, minces about in a mocking fashion.*

GEORGE *laughs.*

GEORGE and **CHLOE** *drink more Lambrini.*

Eat an entire Viennetta with their fingers.

CHLOE *hands* **GEORGE** *several mementos of his relationship: A pic of him and his ex together, a T-shirt which reads 'Best Boyfriend Ever' and a teddy holding a love heart.*

GEORGE *chops each item up with a big pair of scissors and throws them in the bin.*

CHLOE *suddenly produces a can of lighter fluid and skooshes it all over the items, getting quite a bit down her and George's front.*

She takes out a box of matches and tries to strike one.

GEORGE *wrestles it off her.*

GEORGE *and Chloe take it in turns to eat from a huge carton of ice-cream with a big spoon.*

CHLOE *is hogging it.*

GEORGE *smears ice-cream on her nose.*

They have an ice-cream fight.

GEORGE *and* **CHLOE** *lie side by side, full of Lambrini and ice-cream, in the mess they have created.*

They steal glances at one another, giggle, hold hands.

It is ever so slightly awkward.

CHLOE: Still can't get over it. I mean, by text? Seriously, who does that?

GEORGE: Yeah, well. It is what it is.

CHLOE: And to you of all people.

GEORGE: What do you mean by that?

CHLOE: Nothing. It's just like…you're the best person ever, mate.

GEORGE: Do you really think that?

CHLOE: Yeah. Totally.

Silence.

GEORGE: Hmm. Funny.

CHLOE: Funny?

GEORGE: Yeah. I was gonna say the same thing about you.

CHLOE: Haha bullshit.

GEORGE: No really. Really I was.

CHLOE: Really?

GEORGE: Yeah.

Beat.

They look at each other.

CHLOE: That's nice.

GEORGE: Yeah, it is rather. Yeah.

They move closer to each other.

Suddenly, to both of their surprise, they kiss.

The kiss lasts for about five seconds.

They both pull away simultaneously.

Beat.

GEORGE: uuuurgh!

CHLOE: Bleeeeurgh!

GEORGE: Gross! No offence but! Yuckyuckyuck!

CHLOE: *(Wiping at her tongue.)* Pah!Pah!Pah!Pah!

They sit in silence.

GEORGE: Let's…uh…let's agree not to ever do that again, yeah.

CHLOE: Agreeed! That felt…totally weird!

They look at each other.

Laugh.

They are suddenly comfortable with each other again.

They lie back.

CHLOE: Shame though.

GEORGE: Yeah. 'Tis a shame. Tis.

Silence.

GEORGE: Love you, Chloe.

CHLOE: Love you too, George.

LOVE BITE #16

The Dun Law windfarm.

ERICA *enters with a chain and a padlock. She is wearing ear protectors. When animated or stressed she touches her ear, hums quietly and makes a very slight rocking motion to calm herself.*

ERICA: They want to shut you down, y'know? They're all ganging up on you. Making a petition to have you gotten rid of. Listen to this mate.

ERICA *takes a letter from her pocket.*

ERICA: To whom it may concern, We, the residents in the vicinity of the Dun Law Windfarm, are writing an open letter of complaint to Borders council in regards to the obnoxious noise pollution and terrible eyesore which we are forced to put up with twenty-four hours a day.
I, Marjory Tweed, head of 'MANW(OL)F', Mothers Against Noisy Wind (*Onshore Located*) Farms, write to you demanding the immediate closure of these hellish contraptions that not only rape our ears with their constant whirring but also tarnish our views of the rustic borders landscape. The noise of these of these obscene machines can only be described as the sound which a gaggle of geese would make if forced feet first into a large industrial woodchipper. One young mother even claims that when taking her six-month-old to visit her parent's south of the border, the child scream the place down as, having been subjected to this dreadful cacophony ceaselessly since birth, silence now seems loud.
MANWOLF's ranks are growing stronger and now with more than one thousand signatures it would be wise that the council heeds our demands. Clean energy is all well and good…so long as it isn't an annoyance.

I'm so sorry you had to hear that. But I needed to warn you. Don't listen to all those nasty things they've been saying about you. I think you're lovely. And you don't make a 'dreadful cacophony'…you sound beautiful. Like an angel in a helicopter…or what God would sound like if he was a builder…mixing cement in the sky. And you're not an eyesore. You're a big, silver, giant striding across the hills, singing. I remember when I was wee I used to come up here with Dad and I'd stand at you're base and look up at you. And when I did I got this strange feeling in my brain, like you were far too big and I was far too tiny and that the sky was going to pick me up and throw me. I loved that feeling.

I can't let them get rid of you. I don't know what I'd do if you went. You're a part of who I am now…

Don't worry. I won't let them take you away. I've made my own petition. Got three signatures. Me, Dad and Crusher. Crusher's our collie. She slobbered all over it so in a way she sort of signed it.

Thinks for a bit.

To be honest the petition might not work. So I have another plan.

Chains herself to the wind turbine.

So now if MANWOLF wanna get you they're gonna have to get through me!

Pause.

I'll die before I'll let them get you.

Pause.

Which might be sooner rather than later. I forgot to bring my packed lunch.

Pause.

I should probably go get my packed lunch first.

She unties himself.

Don't go anywhere.

Goes to leave.

Love you windfarm!

She exits.

We hear the sound of council lorries approaching. The wirring of the windfarms grinds to a halt.

LOVE BITE #17

Princes Street Gardens. A bench. 4:04pm.

SHY BOY *is lying on the bench looking shagged out and completely stunned with his hair a mess, shirt untucked, ice cream everywhere.* **PHONE GIRL** *looks unscathed and emotionless. She is still texting.*

SHY BOY *sits up.*

SHY BOY: I love you.

She ignores him.

SHY BOY: *(Louder.)* I LOVE YOU!

Silence.

SHY BOY: I'm sorry.

She ignores him.

SHY BOY: I can't help it.

SHY BOY *slaps himself around the head furiously for a bit.*

SHY BOY: Ow.

Silence.

He gets up to leave.

PHONE GIRL *sends her text.* **SHY BOY**'s *phone goes off. He reads the text.*

SHY BOY: Oh.

SHY BOY *walks slowly back and sits on the bench looking blissfully happy.*

SHY BOY: You could have said.

Back on the bench with Malcolm and Cupid.

MALCOLM: Is that everything?

CUPID: What do you mean 'is that everything?' Of course it's not everything. There's millions more happening everywhere all the time.

If I tried to show you them all, your tiny little mind would pop like a piece of bubble wrap. But do you see what's wrong? Is it any wonder I'm crying on a bench? I'm clearly a failure.

MALCOLM: I don't think you're a failure. You're a hot mess but you're definitely not a failure.

CUPID: How so?

MALCOLM: I mean, look at them all. Sure, some of them were awkward, some of them were cringey, some of them were sad and unrequited and some of them were just plain weird. But at least there was… y'know…love there…I think…of one kind or another. I mean, not exactly to a fairytale standard but 'hey' who wants that?

CUPID: Me! I want that. Cos I can't see the love anymore. All I see now is the fumblings, the 'um's and the ah's, the inadequacies, the pain, all that stuff. And…It wears me out. Once, just once, I'd like to see something go, like, full fairytale. But 'hey', like I said, it never does.

MALCOLM: Oh I don't know…

CUPID: Really? Give me one example of something truly romantic that you've seen tonight. Just one.

MALCOLM: Hm.

Silence.

MALCOLM: How about when I gave you my chips?

CUPID: You're confusing romance with pity. You saw a drunken waste of space blubbering all over the pavement and gave them a chip cos it was well awkward. That is all.

MALCOM: No…no actually. I saw the most lovely person I'd ever clapped eyes on looking like they'd had the worst day of their life. And I knew there was probably nothing I could do but I wanted to help somehow so I did the only thing I could think of which was offer them a chip.

Pause.

CUPID: Is that true?

MALCOLM: Yes. Yes it is actually.

Silence.

CUPID: Oh. That's actually quite nice.

Silence.

MALCOLM: Sooo…do you… like me back?…a bit? Or at all? No pressure. Just, y'know, checkin'.

CUPID *laughs sheepishly.*

MALCOLM: Oh come on! I thought with you of all people it wouldn't be awkward.

CUPID: Sorry. It's just no one's ever asked me that before.

MALCOLM: Well.

CUPID: It's sweet of you Malcolm, but you're a teenage boy and I'm an ancient god…would it really work out?

MALCOLM: How do you know my name?

CUPID: I'm a god honey, I'm omniscient. Omniscience doesn't make for good relationships. I'd know what you were doing…all the time. Would you really want that?

MALCOLM: Dunno. 'Spose not.

Awkward silence.

MALCOLM: Well. I better be getting home. Was lovely to meet you… Cupid.

CUPID: Lovely to meet you too, Malcolm.

MALCOLM *begins to walk away.*

CUPID: Balls to it.

CUPID *shoots* **MALCOLM** *in the arse with an arrow then stabs herself with one.*

Then **MALCOLM** *turns and they run in slow motion to each others' arms. They kiss.*

End.

www.salamanderstreet.com

Lightning Source UK Ltd.
Milton Keynes UK
UKHW020340050921
389926UK00008B/617